Stand in Old Light

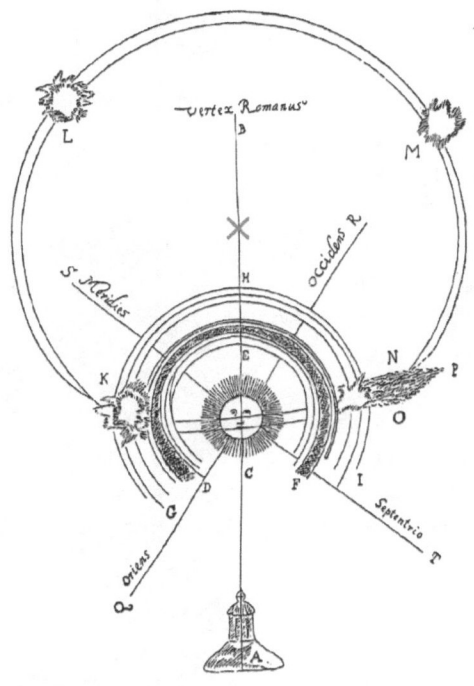

Poems by Matthew Porubsky

Spartan
Press

Spartan Press
Kansas City, Missouri

Spartan
Press

Copyright © Matthew Porubsky, 2024
First Edition: 1 3 5 7 9 10 8 6 4 2
ISBN: 978-1-958182-76-5
LCCN: 2024942145
Cover image: Jon Lee Grafton
Title page image: Rene Descartes?
Author photo: Bita Porubsky

Acknowledgments

Special thanks go to the editors of the following publications where these poems first appeared:

Rose Red Review, Zingara Poets, Honest Publishing, FLARE: The Flagler Review, Futures Trading, Coal City Review, Dream Noir, Melted Butter Magazine, ARC Journal, Sons and Daughters Literary Journal, WIREWORM, Ink In Thirds, Thorny Locust.

Thanks to Brian Daldorph, Jeff Tigchelaar, Sarah Garber Pratte, and Justin Runge for reading these poems over the years and for their continuing support. Thanks to my family for their patience and encouragement. And to Sylvia, Oliver, and Cyrus – thank you, thank you, thank you. And Bita – thank you, dear.

Thanks to Jason Ryberg and Spartan Press for the belief and refinement of these poems.

Table of Contents

for

my family –
the balance they give

"my eyes have seen what my hand did."

–Robert Lowell

I.

*

                Shoreline
fashioned   by heat.

Waves behind – hidden,
                        still.
            My tunic is clean,
white with red trim, buckled at my waist.

How can the horizon be so many lines?

            They are as close as gray
                    is to black
                    is to white.

Creation
                            sits;
a soft smell of sun.
            Each facet –
                    the rim of a cup.

            Each crease –
a fish over the rim of a cup.

I will sleep soon,

                        rest my head on sand.

Wake me at the right moment;
                when the fish is ready to speak.

*

Nothing but   happenings.

     Creation
slowly shows wolves
         in the weeds
         with wet teeth.

Each one mine –

            a pack

     tracking,
         pursuing,
ever-howling
low.

I do not fear   the sounds or steps.

I wait for them – look into their mouths
     for meat,
     for dreams,
     for what should be.

         I let go.

The wolves rest; clover bends below
         a circle of crescent repose.

     Should someone approach,
the wolves' eyes will spark,
         flash like white roses,
         strike like mountain peaks.

*

Hover
    heart-like.

Rain steps from clouds –
blue-silver swords to air.

I clean windowpanes
    with newspaper,
    foam,
    circles.

Vinegar and ink
talc my grip.

Drops of water   pepper the outside,
    gather in corners
        where I edge paper
        to catch soap remnants.

My arm is asleep.

How can the clouds appear as one?
    I know there are at least three,
    perhaps four.
    No. Three. I'm sure.

I can see their edges,
    see how they join to the rain,
    see how they stab through my heart.

*

We bend voices
daily.
Match moody
atmospheres;
a trembling scale.

Without a word, I slip below the curtain,
between two pillars.

Creation
auras in my wake:

viewed by all but me,
embraced in all but me.

My right foot, white-socked,
rests on your marble slab,
taps.

I have eleven shadows
in certain light –

a gradient of reds.

They stretch when needed.

*

Creation has wings.
Today, above the long road, the sun is an oval.

Let me pour you a drink,
   share water
   between cups as if it could float in midair.

I like the way you bend
your index fingers and thumbs together.

Did you know there's no proper top to a triangle?
    It is the same as a circle,
      same as a square.

    Wet your lips to the water;
    there is no dirt smell,
    no plastic at all.

Thank you for the loaf of bread,
    its scent glowing like a halo.

It's like having the sun on a cutting board.
    Keep the knife.
    It is as gentle as you.

Target the right spots on the loaf.

    Show me where to cut each to a slice.

*

Warblers throb their calls.

         Weeds
         desperately sprawl sunward.

You pin me in the doorway with a stare
              as if you have six omniscient eyes.
              I have one;
                  a pink, sleepless one.

         What if you could see with your teeth?
         Vaseline them as if dancing on stage,
              always staring a hard, white smile
                  while spinning in place.

I cannot rearrange your eyes.

         They are set.
         I should be   asleep.

Instead, I am outnumbered –
         fighting off dreams as if on a ledge
         with opponents to each side.

Let the birds hop from limb to   limb.

The high ground is no help.

*

Touch   when able:
opening   doors,
bumps   in the kitchen,
feet   under bar tables,
eyes.

      The sunflowers are beyond decoration –
           more like   oxygen,
                         light,
                         lion's mane.

Your cat walks by fast as a glance strangers share.
Needles in my eyes
           slim the skin   beneath your robe.

There's a vague smell of pollen,
               of leaves blending sunlight.

         Feel me unmasked, wrung-out.

You look over the pyramids in your mind,
      sit as if upside-down.
        Your skin glows from who has touched you –
              some posed lion,
              some growing stem.

We are not like pictures.
We are the negatives;   exposure blinding
us thin.

*

Don't go to sleep.
Don't go to sleep.

> I'll create,

>> hang it up, display:

a moon with closed eyes,
pieces of eight in shallow water.

> I'm a jumble of rough
> steps.

You can sift me,   knead me,
      bake me as bread.

Help me rise,

>> nourish small mouths again

> before the coming sojourn.

Just upturn my cup.
Just clasp my cloak.
> Whisper me a shape for these stars.

*

My hands have glowed on several occasions.
It's in no way a divine glow,
       but enough to light the stairs to the cellar,
       enough to read by.

I can live buried,
learn to breathe like a worm.

       I'll help the grass grow.

I'll be loose enough
              to aerate, to slide through.

       My hands will help light the evergreens
           on moonless nights –
           bioluminescent twinge
           to call the moths.

Use the branches and leaves
       to laurel who you'd like.

I'll be below.

*

We both stare.

Five white petals stretch like a pentagram,
                      yellow center circle,
crowning from six golden cups.

You fix them,

                  line them exact.

Your creation is perfection
            as much as creation.

                  Step back.
                  Stop.
                  Re-exact.

You ask how I can just stand there.

                  Re-exact.
                  Re-exact.

I step forward:
                  bend at knees,
                  bend at neck,
                  bend to smell.

We are each staring at something else.

*

Which should I wear   today?
        Pill-face,
        drink-face,
        sleep-face,
        face.   All fit tight.

Let's put them   together.

        See
noses
        flattened,
ears
        layered mute,
eyes glazed
        to eyes   to eyes.

So   many   mouths.

        This is no face.

        Beneath:
a skull,
        dry sockets,   teeth

        waiting for
some kind of vision,
some kind of skin.

*

> Daughter,
> the stars are taking shape.
> Do you see?
> Do you see the tree
> > there?
> > And here.

There is no fog of light so far out.
> Can you smell the grapevines on the wind?

> Daughter, look!
There, the constellation Mercy.
It connects to Beauty to the north,
> Foundation to the south.

> Follow
> > your finger across eastward.
Do you see how Severity and Understanding
> line up, like a pillar?

> > > The real secret —
> you can fashion all this as you choose,

design your choices as they appear to you.

> Do this and you will never smell rust.
> The breeze that wakes you will be gentle.
Your domain will be lush
> with creation.

*

        Son.
You sit with the look
           of a lonesome god.
      The juggle of   infinity

      is disorienting, at first:

      like a ship in high waves,
      like gripping stars.

        Son,
your   hair is   trimmed
      and so much   darker than mine.

      Do you hear the wind over the lake?

      Soon,
           you'll handle all this.

Waves will still wave,
stars will still call,

        but you'll toss them hand to hand,
      breath steady, slow,

      as you stand on one foot.

*

A cloak of water fits me perfectly:
bend of my crown,
roll of my shoulders,
house of my body.

This is how we hug –
if that's what it could be called.
Closing eyes helps vision
what isn't there.

Your arms go straight through.
Or do mine go straight through?

We wait for it to end.

Creation,
a gold chalice,
can be held with one hand
and admired with the other.

You could whisper something shiny.
Instead, you put your ear to a shell,
chant ocean salt and song.

My chair
moves closer to the waterline,
sinks on the left side.

My cloak
joins the glimmer;
takes me along.

*

Lay my body   out.

       Begin recording incisions.
View
       what has changed from birth.

              I have been born
                     many times.
Each
       rearranges
          my insides.

Its mush-paste
       sticks, holds fast.

Wear a mask,   gloves.
       Recite what you see.
       Weigh.
       Catalogue.

       Carve me as your sculpture.

I'll have my eyes   closed.

*

        Truth
        in my fingernails

grows   dirty.

I clip them in unstrung bows.

My creation:
        a mound of trees,
        naked clouds,
        a sunset.

All this clear at their very tips.

        Watch them read, write, honey.

They'll grow when I'm dead.

Recall   where they used to
                slide.

*

Darling,
let's look back to our garden,
vibrant with light and leaves,
fruits   fashioning   in symmetry.

Can we share bodies still?
Has it always been given?
Not shared?

You are a pale envelope opening,
a filled Ball Jar cracking.

My knuckles are strong for you.

Darling,
I see scales   on the plants,

skins like tar   separating
them from sun.

We kiss blistered lips,
lose balance,
hear the push of thunder.

II.

*

I drive to walk
        desert heat.

        Unknown panhandles –
                        nothing but braided fences,
                        hot slaughter smell,
                        rabbits rushing from headlights.
They feed to dark
        New Mexico.

I climb
elevation
        black lit.

Sun over bulbous blue rocks
        becomes Arizona;
one single star sign emitting   light.

                There is space in hours, too.
I climb down swerving   mountain roads
                        to forest
                        to desert.

                I search for sand.

*

Drive-think   time –
          moving through space,
          constellations streak,
radiate continuous playouts.

          Oh darling,
another dead deer
          on the side
          of the road,
another armadillo
          split open.

          What is their judgement?
      How loud is the trumpet
          that conjures their weeping coda?

          I'm a dart.
Winds   whistle
          through my feathers.

          My shiniest point rusted.

  Dust wakes thick from   desert roads,
          boils my movement
          with rolling clouds.

*

Hurtling toward the sun,

constellations   shape   solid –
                                                       not there to see.
          Looking a certain way,

                    mountain-clouds
                                        are not shore,
                         range of rocks
                                        are not sand.

I transfigure   double vision –
head shake   to one view.

          Stars pop away,   disappear distant.

               I capture the desert to wake myself,
                         watch sand soak
                                   into my hand.

Thirst begins like a naked branch.

                              It all flakes away
                    into my shadows stacked as
          one beneath my feet.

＊

Sister,
how do you rise up
from the grains,
dressed in yellow and oxblood,
to gaze at me
as if to give shelter?

I become a bird,
perch on the knuckle
of your index finger,
chirp for water.

Your gentle arms flex.

Do you see   the coyote,
gray with curling tail,
in its long sleep
at your feet?

Me.

The snail, lost
in the sand,
closing into its shell.

Again, me.

Will you
turn down my bed,
enable the slightest solace?

Will you conjure olives,
share them raw and bitter
so I learn how to wait?

*

      Under
          Palo Verde trees,
skinny
as short
birch,
      I smoke
in lilting
fern shade.

          Squat cacti
          tombstone the wavy expanse.

          The White Tank Mountains
          grit in the distance;
          carve the sky.

              Two mourning doves,
              skirt from
a branch;
              the only birds I've seen in days.

No cloud in the sky.

          They part directions in a swoop.

*

This desert is layered in horizontal convections.

Walking the path,
      I recite mathematical formulas:
              inequalities,
              fractions,
              less than,
              equal to.

I travel to old births, resets.
Transmogrification of flesh for flesh.

All seem like gaining lift beneath clipped wings;
      a series of piled swords.

I'm a surveyor of lines,
rewriter of scenes.

I grip a hot rock:
      solid, burning.
      I smell the resin of a history in heat.
Formulas activate within.

          I float,
      leave not tracks –
      dangle linear as if waking slowly.

*

A pit near the path aches with remains:

handgun, shotgun shell casings
   scattered in piles,
    broken glass reveals from sand
      like snow-covered peaks,
    sun-dyed aluminum
      with muted branding.

Cacti shadows act as an audience.

    There was sweat in their grip,
      whoever held those
      beers and guns.

    There was adrenalin, hot and cold,
      as they watched shots
      splash dust, arc unseen.

I dodge a rattlesnake den.
    I see the snake stare.

It speaks to me, tells me a story –
    bullets waking it from a peaceful sleep,
    missing it by a scale,
    resonating on the tips of its tongue.

*

I wish to fight   the sun.
                    Glorious battle:
                              heat,

radiation,
          my creation.

Rivals   to the last,
we   battle with
             bared teeth,

slings of energy,

                         waves,

burst of what's inside.

Burned to   bruises,
                  we both subside,

converse about gravity –

                  how long until
                           the final

explosion,   our universes expanding to a split,

                  the darkness   after.

*

Uncle,
>
> you must not know you're dead.
> I can't blame you
>> with a sunset this gradient –
>> shining through you like ice in whiskey.
> Without separation,

how are you supposed to know much of anything?

Even I could be the dead one.
I could be dead.

>
> Give me a sign –

draw a circle in the sand,
conjure the aroma of lilies.
>> Tap that rock to release wine.

>> We lap up the puddles
>>> as if elk resting in a glade
>>> after outrunning the hunt.
>> You are the one that's bleeding,

a limp finally appearing
in the relief of escape.
>> You stop drinking first,
>>> watch the stars blink into form,
>>> kneel to repose, then recline.
>> You watch me drink.
>>> I blur as you close your eyes,
>>> grunt to yourself that it is only sleep
>>> covering your wounds.

*

Shucked
        from my skin,
        the pulp of me melts
                beside scrub grass,
figures to   rocks and shells.

        I see a face   in the sands –
        a reflection   in the lake.

           The snakes
                remember me,
                whisper,
"Brother,   listen! Brother!"

        I change forty days
                to one.

        I have slimmed
        from the fast;
        created a battle-fresh
                transfiguration.

I glow from burns,
                pulse in the edging night.

        My pockets stuffed
        with new poise,

        I cup a flint box in my hands –
        gently blow against potential,

        wait for a flame.

*

I wrap   myself in eons.

        Space and time
                    are mine:
        my lantern in the blackness,
        my cloak against the cold.

                Traveling forward
                        is the same as
                traveling backward.

        It's all about what light
                you let yourself see.

I bend with unseen forces,
        watch myself curve,
                        hollow,
                        refract.

        I let myself see the orbits
                slipped from.

        I let myself see the skins
                slipped from.

The lantern leads itself.

        I am like the light
                        scuttling
                in all directions.

*

I leave
before the storm –
bulb-heads
over the shore-like
Estrella Mountains.

Lightning amplifies in elevation.
Strikes in the
forest
send up smoke,   flame-licks.

Higher,

I see a city of lights.
Higher,

rain melts tarmac.
Higher,

I descend through
night,
wake to the light of calm plains,
see another storm in the distance –

a funnel cloud spinning
where it pleases.

III.

*

Watch the way
          existence continues.

     Sky and stream
     ripple the same blue.

     Sprigs fold from
     limbs to tremble
     sun and wind.

Smoke in the air
     reminds that it's time to burn,

time for ash to rise.

     What kind of arrows
     fly through the immovable?

     What is it that holds us
                    waiting?

          I tap my foot,

     begin to chart
          the length of brevity –

     how it disregards
          miles of creation,

     how it flattens
          a cloudless sky.

*

I get to relive

                    you hot;
          clear spirits from blood.

     The moons on your shoulders
               pull opposite directions,
     crescent you to a split.

     Ghost-story eyes
               continue to deconstruct
anything recognizable.

               This is the new pattern:

               your body falling to lines,
               my eyes drying,
               the cat playing with its tail.

     The castle and walls thin in the distance,
               disappear to a hill, a tall tree.

     I wear a belt that holds nothing.

You shimmy your hips;
          laugh like sun on water.

*

Tenuous grins slate junctions
            when we are together:
leaving,
arriving,
halfway there.

You've rearranged,
            like the scent of dyed hair.

I haven't told you –
            I've learned to hold swords by their blades,
                        several at once.
            I can slide them down my throat,
                        slide them up my throat –
the taste of steel like butter.

My creation
            slinks, shoulders my neck,
            winks while I try to shove it in pockets.

The swords are easier than greetings;
same ol',
                        same ol'
oil in pores.

*

Cramp in pleasantry.

Pleases, pleas
come easy.

This look:

       solid fracture in air,
       fire crackling like a stream over stones.

My compete complete;
       creation pests between us.

       You're a sway of wind.
       I'm a desert rock.

Lift across me,
see masks burning
       with shadows.

Admire my new shirt.

*

       I want to
       fall
       hard,
smell your   deep   deeply.

Give me a slim to fill, darling.
       Let me climb your
       pinions,
humble to you
       deconstruction.

       I'll place a star
       below each of my feet,
       one above my head.
       Hold the last circled in my arms
       as if it were the moon.

A black cloak will cover us both.

       Autonomy
       manifests physically from this

       like towers rising from
       neighboring cities.

Drawn lines are easiest to see
       in the dark;

       they can be almost anything.

*

Labyrinth thoughts
    wring like white marble.

    My sons,
    my daughter
            laugh,
splash mud that mixes
        with raindrops
    on their clothes, their faces.

        Home is a

                flashpoint -
                sparkless

    burning.

    I don't see the rainbow
        until they tell me.

They fling mud as high as they can.

    I don't tell them
    the rainbow is just in our eyes,
    not actually in the sky.

    I grab a handful of mud,
    throw along with them,

all of us adding
    a color each of us needs.

*

In the yard,
I stretch upwards, reach my arms to spearpoint,
            hands palm to palm.

            My skin grains to smooth wood,
                        veining dark from light.
            A crouching frog forms
                        below my knees,
                        eyes and mouth curve wide.
            My left side carves
                        to a downward facing sword,
                        right side to a staff with living sprigs.
            Between the two, my thighs
                        shape to overlapping circles,
                        vesica piscis touching to a center.
            Ouroboros, mouth to tail,
                        belts my waist below.
            My chest and back mirror each other –
                        a series of distancing arches,
                        hallways to a mountain range
                        with a sun rising.
            Shoulders silhouette:
                        bull, angel, lion, eagle.
            My arms fan to owl's wings,
                        horns feather above gaping eyes,
                        never blinking or
                        never opening.

*

When you first saw me,
I was upside down, as if hung by the ankle.

You told me once,
when I was born,
you saw a slight halo around my head,
        but that could have been
        from your loss of blood.

Mother,

                you were my first mask,
                my initial drink of enlightenment –
                softest milk and touch.

        When I was bound inside you,
                I recall seeing a shine;
                muted light glittering
                the liquids of you to swirl
                deep, starry, and calm.

What if it wasn't the flashlight like you told me?
What if that was the closest we
                ever have been to creation?

The timeline branches electric from that point.

        Mother,
                unscab my eyes; help me see
the correspondence inside and out.

Retie the rope, pull back my bed.

*

    Spiders in trees build,
    salvage
        what they can
from a creation
        more empty than full –
    live on what snags, sticks
            just enough.

    Under-leaves
    lift pale,
        reveal what's hidden.

Our connection is a web
        in wind,
    billowing in pulses,

    catching nothing to spin,
        nothing to funnel existence.

*

Old friend,

how do you spell your name?
What is this laugh
that was once a cry?

I have a chart here.

It maps our stories
for you to review –
so we are on the same page.

Yes, the lines aren't supposed
to slant like that.
Those   are traces,

the shuck and silks of corn:
slick, sticky, crisp.

That's how I remember your eyes,
how I carry your breaths in a bindle.

Have this rose
before I take my last step.
I'm many shadows
layered to one:
a revelation of sun,
a step from the rocks.

*

Phantom
          obsessions
cling to your hems;
      vacillate our polarities.

You sew
     with agile perfection,
     as if touching yourself
          while someone watches.

          Your patching dovetails.

          Mine overlaps, ironed on.

     You stretch thread,
        moisten it
        to eye the needle.

I'm pulled close for a moment.

          We feel something:
        murmuration of wheat in a field,
        support of a receiving pillow.

     You humble distractions.
        Stitch tight enough

        and there is no need to twist a knot.

*

Father,
             you can't sleep either?

             Giving up spiraling sheets
                          for grapes.
Steps are shadows in the dark –
             your footfalls soft enough to not
                          slip through.

You've built trains
             for years in the dark,
             coupling car to car to locomotive,
constructing surges
             of the horizontal god.

             Your skin is moon and rust,
                  even in this light.

You tell me how you learn
                  to see without lanterns,
                  practice opossum-wide eyes,
                  walk night for day.

             It takes trust in the rocks underfoot,
                  acceptance of light's limits,
                  sureness in self,

                  not unlike the stairs –
                  in stillness, each step leads
                  where it must.

*

The tower
    is a gargle of words.

Each builder's tongue
        set to fire —
    fresh syllables gag in throats,
            flick off tips.

        There is no strike of lightning,
           no fall from great heights.

    Confusion.
    Walking away.
    Restarting.

    Each begin to gather
        their own stones,

    level them for a sturdy base.

IV.

*

Voice has no filter.
Water on the boat side
        is quiet as a spring font.

Breath is absent of smoke.

Magma cools,
        takes soil, seed —
                learns what is needed for growth.

        Your ears curve in math:
ancient, receiver width.

        An aplomb of full wind
                helps the skiff
                glide through water and ice.

It is graspable between   fingers.

        The pilot sings,
fashions us union strong,
                pushes his tall wand through depth.

        Squeeze my hand again;
        look what's there
        silhouetted at the shoreline.

*

I'm waiting,
        the vines taking to my toes –
exposed to what happens.

       There is no skin left
              to shed, to shake loose
to be discovered by the next
             who passes by.

       Tendrils weave me,
             wreath my body and hair,

ornament me outside what is inside.

       I am fit for a hearth.
       I am fit for a grave.
       I am fit.

*

So   many
          maybes
everything   becomes   blue.

The guards are like trees,

          feathered   together
                           holding
                           to the meadow.

          Pines lace the open air.

Sing
to limbs   old songs;
          cradle mountains
          in the entryway.

Fashion
a harp from sticks;
          play mementos again.

The way
          your eyes   look   longer

show me as a shadow.

          If we step away,
          we will see how ardent
                    the garden truly is.

*

I am dressed
     in fire.

          You haven't seen yet,
               haven't seen the way
     I walk like a pillar of clouds
            through the desert.

    The bed is skeletal:

          frame of ribs,
          spindle legs,
          hollow-eyed pillows.

The coil of you is
          tight; self-compressing
                autonomy
          your cinch of creation.

    I try   to slip through,
          promises soft as spits of flame.

*

I act
as monster
from a show —
they laugh,   run
in game,
pepper the yard with light.

You see me clearly.
Something they miss.

From the parapet,
I can hold this creation
like a globe,
roll it in my hand,
in sunlight,

watch the visions bend,
shine clear.

I observe the sea
carving lines,
courtyards rounding off
fences,
meadows growing dense.

My distance is as
fitting as rain to soil.

*

Same body,
        alternate life.

Your curves   continue;
                   flux at image of old
                   in new language.

There's a ghost for each of us
looming behind.
Winks register nothing but closed eyes.

Specters don't hold hands.
                   They haunt like noxious fumes,
                   taunt our new selves not to touch,
                   not to hover near for too long.

The air is broken tile.

We walk cautiously with slippery feet.

*

Fringe of contact;
> we shore up
> even-tide.

Earth,   sky
> eyes
link in this slip,   anchor to beach
> concrete.

> Dilated hunger,
> black circles

opening to alternate
casts.

> This lizard chases, bites its own tail.
> That lion roars flame,
> > chest arcing with breath.

Meeting again is a
> bloom:
> heart speed,
> solar flare,
> tree shade.

An instant is   long,
> enough to

> sprout
> seed.

*

I trace

        your constellation,
        take you as notes,
        fit on the mask you give me.

      Our paralleled
        vision
            displaces connection.

      Oppression of carrying a weight
                swells as
      constitution shakes, wary to press on.

Sticks bundled together
        have a strength,
    become unbreakable.

I'll burn them in the garden,

      let the ashes
        fold into the ground.

Later, I will dig   down to the clay,

      use a handful
    to shape a body,
        rounded limbs and
        sagging head.

      I will leap in.

*

We are a nature collage
       decoupaged on paper,
sealed   down   slick.

Image of once growths.

A variety of leaves,
       still for the viewing.

Magnet it to the refrigerator –
       admire it for a short time.

File it to box storage.

Rediscover the plastered arrangement –
       admire it moments less.

       Return it to piles.

*

Forget
                the flow of traffic.
Sink your hands   in dirt,
black at your cuticles.
                Dig
        a new hole to house
old seeds,
                regrets,
                creations.

                Include
        a strand of hair,
        a smooth rock,
        a scrap of paper
                with your name written
                three times horizontally,
                three times vertically.

Once covered,
                the first night of a new moon,

        the image of you flickers above,
        movements jerking and silent
        as if projected from eight-millimeter film.

        You blur in and out of focus,
        cartwheel and jump,
        jolt in dark and light,
        close-up to a mute smile,
        stick out your tongue,

        cut out.

*

Skin   lives   slick.

Two   new   bodies

      sprout alongside air,
twine places,
space places.
      Foliage crisp   green.
      Roots in   dark matter.
Forms of shade
          chronological.

         Shadows still for now.

    My choice of duality
         so plain.

One with braids   tight.
One with hair   wild.

    The answer is always in the distance:

        pyramids echoing stars,
        dunes reciting winds.

I put my arms out
        to the sides;
        step forward.

*

We are our secrets.

Look at us to scale –
        live, like lattices full of vines.

The charge into the wind
        streaks with action;
        bends trees,
        blows birds sideways
        at the mercy of sky.

My legs stretch with each stride.
        I raise my sword.
My song is as thin as stratus clouds,
        my armor as present.

I dream of rest by a campfire:
        ash in my hair,
        smoke in my eyes.

*

Preparation to hold a star begins slowly,
        as if your horse is tired,
        heavy with supplies.

You will not need a glove.
Soak your hand in a salve
mixed of blue comfrey,
        orange calendula,
        water.

Scoop the star in your open palm –
        the light's texture crisp as aged paper.

Its glow changes,
        blends to a sky of rising sun.

        Creation rests beside you:
        new skin, quiet mind.

Hold it, only for a few moments,
view seconds tumble into years.

Then, gently place the star into the salve,
watch water luminesce.

A horizon at the surface glows without end.

*

You comb your hair,
        braid it tight.

      Twists and overlays
          hold each strand.
          Nothing is left unstructured.

          We are paralleled –
          distance continuous.

It is simple to stare at what has been spilled,
forget the full cups at our backs.

There are three arches below the bridge.
        From here, we can only see two.

        The stream will never stop.
It has enough room to continue
          smooth, gently sounding
          calm to travelers, children to sleep,

        filling any space in need of occupancy.

*

Secrets are like swords driven
in the ground blade first,
        menhir slicing wind.

Enough of them can line as a wall,
        fence one side from another.

Can I tell time from their shadows?
What is left after their slow, dark cuts?

                If one of us were blindfolded,
                these secrets would be scents:
                        charcoal ash, saffron rice.

New webs in doorways
        pattern the mysteries together.

Standing back
        you can see how it all works together,
        how it pulses from things unseen.
Up close,
        two strands cross, feign ignorance.
Inside,
        you're bound,
struggle until twisted absolute,
wait for blood to drain.

*

There will be a night with no shadows,

see each other's   constellations,
        smell bread   almost.

Find a pulse   of something
nearly there.

       Sit, listen
           alone.

          Pile the relics.
       Pack them tight if this night
comes again.

Enter through new doors,
shoulder years,

          stand in old light,

            fly.

Matthew Porubsky is a writer born and raised in Topeka, Kansas. He is the author of *voyeur poems*, *Fire Mobile (the pregnancy sonnets)*, *John*, *Ruled by Pluto*, and *Serpent's Lap*. He currently works as a copywriter at the University of Kansas. Read more poetry at matthewporubsky.com.

This project was made possible, in part, by generous support from the Osage Arts Community.

Osage Arts Community provides temporary time, space and support for the creation of new artistic works in a retreat format, serving creative people of all kinds — visual artists, composers, poets, fiction and nonfiction writers. Located on a 152-acre farm in an isolated rural mountainside setting in Central Missouri and bordered by ¾ of a mile of the Gasconade River, OAC provides residencies to those working alone, as well as welcoming collaborative teams, offering living space and workspace in a country environment to emerging and mid-career artists. For more information, visit us at www.osageac.org

Osage Arts Community